Bartlett Public Library

YA NF
34.25

D1061282

J11.0.0268
L116N

DISCARD

THE NUREMBERG TRIALS

LAURA LA BELLA

ROSEN PUBLISHING®

New York

Published in 2015 by The Rosen Publishing Group, Inc.
29 East 21st Street, New York, NY 10010

Copyright © 2015 by The Rosen Publishing Group, Inc.

First Edition

All rights reserved. No part of this book may be reproduced in any form without permission in writing from the publisher, except by a reviewer.

Library of Congress Cataloging-in-Publication Data

La Bella, Laura, author.
The Nuremberg Trials/Laura La Bella.
    pages cm.—(A documentary history of the Holocaust)
Includes bibliographical references and index.
ISBN 978-1-4777-7607-0 (library bound)
1. Nuremberg Trial of Major German War Criminals, Nuremberg, Germany, 1945-1946—Juvenile literature. 2. International Military Tribunal—Juvenile literature. 3. War crime trials—Juvenile literature. I. Title.
KZ1176.5.L3 2014
341.6'90268—dc23

2013044028

Manufactured in the United States of America

CONTENTS

INTRODUCTION

Defendants *(front row, left to right)*: Hermann Goering, Rudolf Hess, Joachim von Ribbentrop, Wilhelm Keitel, *(back row, left to right)* Karl Donitz, Erich Raeder, Baldur von Schirach, and Fritz Sauckel sit in court during the International Military Tribunal in Nuremberg.

When Adolf Hitler rose to power in Germany in the 1930s, he ushered in a period of history in which unprecedented atrocities were committed against innocent people. Against the backdrop of World War II, which was fought on six continents and in which Hitler worked to realize his goal for European domination, the Holocaust claimed the lives of an estimated six million Jewish men, women, and children. Throughout Europe, Jews were murdered, wrongfully imprisoned, and tortured. Jewish-owned businesses were targeted and destroyed, and the personal possessions of Jewish families were confiscated.

As World War II came to an end and the horrors of the Holocaust came to light, the international community faced an extraordinary challenge in how to seek justice for criminal and murderous, genocidal behavior on an almost unimaginable scale. The Nazi regime needed to be held accountable. Backed by the governments of the United States, Great Britain, France, and the Soviet Union, the International Military Tribunal was created to bring perpetrators of the Holocaust to justice. Held in Nuremberg, Germany, the International Military Tribunal attempted to bring legal understanding and punishment to the men behind the crimes of the Holocaust.

On October 1, 1946, the International Military Tribunal handed down its verdicts in the trials of twenty-two major Nazi leaders. Eleven were given the death penalty, three were acquitted, three were given life imprisonment, and four were given prison sentences ranging in length from ten to twenty years. Those sentenced to death were hanged at Spandau Prison five days later.

In addition to providing some level of justice to the European Jewish community, the International Military Tribunal forged new ground in international law. It served to define war crimes and crimes against humanity, and it worked to establish a legal precedent for the establishment of a permanent international court of law.

CHAPTER 1

THE RISE OF THE THIRD REICH

In Germany in the early 1930s, the mood was gloomy and desperate. The country had faced a humiliating defeat at the end of World War I. Terms of the Treaty of Versailles, which ended the so-called Great War, forced Germany to accept responsibility for starting the global conflict. As punishment, Germany was forced to pay reparations to Russia, France, and Great Britain—the countries that had banded together and defeated it.

A worldwide economic depression followed in the war's wake, and Germany, in particular, was hit hard. There were no jobs, no factories, and no industry of any kind. Millions of Germans were out of work and struggling to feed their families. The country had little faith in its government, known as the Weimar Republic. The challenging conditions proved to be a fertile atmosphere to foster the rise to power of a little-known German soldier and rabid anti-Semite named Adolf Hitler.

Hitler became the leader of the National Socialist German Workers' Party, better known as the Nazi Party. His charismatic, fiery, angry, spellbinding speeches attracted a wide following of Germans who were eager for change and desperate to find a way

During the depression that followed World War I, millions of Germans were out of work and struggling. Many relied on soup kitchens for food.

out of their hopeless economic struggles. Hitler promised to lead the German people out of economic depression and to restore Germany to its rightful place among Europe's powerful elite. The downtrodden German population believed in his pledge to build a new and glorious Germany. Hitler was appointed chancellor, or head of the German government, on January 30, 1933.

A DICTATOR EMERGES

Hitler's Nazi Party, also known as the Third Reich, quickly stripped German Jews of their basic rights. A day after a suspicious fire at the Reichstag (the German parliament) on February 27, 1933, Hitler's government issued a decree that suspended all civil rights and created a state of emergency in which official decrees could be enacted without parliamentary approval.

Hitler dissolved labor unions, gave the government control over businesses, and banned churches from criticizing the Nazi state. He also used books, radio, literature, paintings, film, and the press as propaganda tools to shape public opinion and spread the Nazi philosophy. Any books that did not support the Nazi agenda were publicly burned. Historians generally agree that agents of the Nazi Party deliberately set the fire at the Reichstag in

Adolf Hitler, who rose to power by promising to return Germany to its rightful place in the world, capitalized on the fears, anxieties, and frustrations of the German people.

order to provide Hitler with a pretext for seizing more governmental control, suspending citizens' rights, and imposing what was essentially martial law.

When German president Paul von Hindenburg died in August 1934, Hitler assumed the powers of the German presidency. The German army swore an oath of personal loyalty to Hitler, and Hitler established himself as Reich president (head of state), Reich chancellor (head of government), and Führer (head of the Nazi Party).

The goals and ideals of the Nazi Party were communicated to the public through propaganda, a strategy Hitler himself wrote about in *Mein Kampf*, a book he authored in 1926. In *Mein Kampf* he wrote, "Propaganda tries to force a doctrine on the whole people... Propaganda works on the general public from the standpoint of an idea and makes them ripe for the victory of this idea." Hitler established a Reich Ministry of Public Enlightenment and Propaganda headed by Joseph Goebbels. The ministry's purpose was to ensure that the Nazi message was successfully communicated through art, music, theater, films, books, radio, educational materials, and the press.

The Ministry of Public Enlightenment and Propaganda attempted, in essence, to brainwash the German people into believing, accepting, and furthering the Nazi point of view. Germans were consistently reminded of the ongoing struggle against their foreign enemies and of presumed Jewish rebellion against authority and civil society. During periods preceding the proposal or adoption of legislation and executive measures against Jews, anti-Semitic propaganda campaigns created an atmosphere that was tolerant of violence against Jews. Propaganda also encouraged ordinary Germans' passive acceptance of increasingly harsh and repressive measures against Jews.

JEWISH PERSECUTION BEGINS

Anti-Semitism and the persecution of Jews represented a central tenet of Nazi ideology. In their twenty-five-point party program, published in 1920, Nazi Party members publicly declared their intention to segregate Jews from "Aryan" society and to revoke Jews' political, legal, and civil rights. During the first six years of Hitler's dictatorship (1933–1939), Jews felt the effects of more than four hundred decrees and regulations that restricted all aspects of their public and private lives. This was done with the intention of compelling Jews to flee the country.

The first of these major laws was the Law for the Restoration of the Professional Civil Service. Established on April 7, 1933, the law stated that all Jewish and politically unreliable civil servants and employees were to be excluded from state service. Additional laws were also enacted that deeply affected the daily life of Jews. Among other things, the new laws:

- Restricted the number of Jewish students at German schools and universities
- Sharply curtailed Jewish participation in medical and legal professions
- Restricted Jewish doctors from being reimbursed with public (state) health insurance funds for their services
- Revoked the licenses of Jewish tax consultants

In addition, Jewish civilian workers were fired from positions within the army, and Jewish actors were forbidden from performing on the stage or on-screen.

THE NUREMBERG LAWS

In 1935, at their annual rally in Nuremberg, Germany, Nazi leaders announced new laws that firmly established many of the racial theories that dominated Nazi ideology. What follows is the text of the first of the two Nuremberg Laws, officially referred to as the "Laws for the Protection of German Blood and German Honor":

Moved by the understanding that the purity of German blood is essential to the further existence of the German people, and inspired by the uncompromising determination to safeguard the future of the German nation, the Reichstag has unanimously resolved upon the following law, which is promulgated herewith:

Section 1
- Marriages between Jews and citizens of German or kindred blood are forbidden. Marriages concluded in defiance of this law are void, even if, for the purpose of evading this law, they were concluded abroad.
- Proceedings for annulment may be initiated only by the Public Prosecutor.

Section 2
- Extramarital sexual intercourse between Jews and subjects of the state of Germany or related blood is forbidden.

Section 3
- Jews will not be permitted to employ female citizens under the age of 45, of German or kindred blood, as domestic workers.

Hitler began to institute the Nuremberg Laws, which served to humiliate and isolate Jews and restrict their involvement in German society. Jews were forbidden to marry or have any sort of romantic relationships with Germans. Those who did, like this Christian woman and Jewish man, were forced to publicly wear signs that announced their indiscretions.

Section 4

- Jews are forbidden to display the Reich and national flag or the national colors.
- On the other hand they are permitted to display the Jewish colors. The exercise of this right is protected by the State.

Section 5

- A person who acts contrary to the prohibition of Section 1 will be punished with hard labor.
- A person who acts contrary to the prohibition of Section 2 will be punished with imprisonment or with hard labor.
- A person who acts contrary to the provisions of Sections 3 or 4 will be punished with imprisonment up to a year and with a fine, or with one of these penalties.

Section 6

- The Reich Minister of the Interior in agreement with the Deputy Führer and the Reich Minister of Justice will issue the legal and administrative regulations required for the enforcement and supplementing of this law.

Section 7

- The law will become effective on the day after its promulgation; Section 3, however, not until January 1, 1936. (Source: The Jewish Virtual Library)

A second law, the Reich Citizenship Law, declared those who were not of German blood to be subjects of the state, whereas so-called Aryans were citizens of the state. Jews, therefore, were effectively stripped of their German citizenship and the rights and protections that went along with it.

Hitler himself introduced the laws in the Reichstag and argued for their necessity in the following chilling terms:

Bitter complaints have come in from countless places citing the provocative behavior of Jews...[W]e have no choice but to contain the problem through legislative measures...This law is an attempt to find a legislative solution....[I]f this attempt fails, it will be necessary to transfer [the Jewish problem] ... to the National Socialist Party for a final solution by law. (Source: The History Place)

The Nuremberg Laws also increased anti-Semitic segregation. Jewish patients were no longer admitted to city- or state-run hospitals in the German city of Düsseldorf. German court judges could not cite legal commentaries or opinions written by Jewish authors. Jewish officers were expelled from the army. Jewish university students were not allowed to sit for doctoral exams. The Reich Propaganda Ministry issued a decree forbidding Jewish soldiers to be named among the dead in World War I memorials.

THE FIRST CONCENTRATION CAMPS

The first concentration camps were established soon after Hitler's appointment as chancellor in 1933. At first they were created to detain both real and perceived political opponents of the Nazi Party and its agenda. The concentration camps held people in harsh conditions with little food and water. Prisoners had no legal rights in Nazi Germany.

German authorities established camps all over Germany to handle the large numbers of people determined by Nazi and Nazi supporters to be a threat to the Third Reich. Prisoners were used as forced labor on construction projects or at coal mines and stone quarries. Camp guards deliberately mistreated prisoners and kept them malnourished. They forced them to work in dangerous conditions, which caused a high rate of death. These camps eventually became the sites for mass killings of Jews and others deemed enemies of Nazi Germany.

ARYANIZATION

"Aryanization" was the formal process of reducing the number of Jewish-owned businesses in Germany. Government agencies at all levels aimed to exclude Jews from the economic sector of German life by preventing them from earning a living. Jews were required to register their domestic and foreign property and assets. This gave the Nazis a list of Jewish-owned goods and possessions they would later forcibly seize to enrich the Reich.

German authorities intended to "Aryanize" all Jewish businesses, which meant removing all Jewish workers and managers. They also sought to transfer all Jewish-owned companies and enterprises to non-Jewish Germans, who bought them at prices purposely fixed well below market value.

THE KRISTALLNACHT POGROM

The Kristallnacht pogrom, also known as the Night of Broken Glass, was a wave of anti-Jewish violence that included rioting, destroying synagogues, and plundering Jewish-owned businesses. On November 9, 1938, violent anti-Jewish demonstrations broke out across Germany, Austria, and the Sudetenland region of Czechoslovakia. These government-sanctioned riots followed the assassination of Ernst vom Rath, a German foreign official who had been shot two days earlier by Herschel Grynszpan, a seventeen-year-old Polish Jew. Grynszpan was distraught over the deportation of his family from Germany. Nazi officials did nothing to stop or control the riots. Instead, they depicted the violence against Jews as a justifiable reaction to the murder of vom Rath.

Damage from the aftermath of Kristallnacht, or the Night of Broken Glass, when rioting targeted many Jewish-owned businesses.

In the aftermath of Kristallnacht, Nazi leaders stepped up their Aryanization efforts and enforced the physical isolation and segregation of all Jews. Barred from all public schools and universities, cinemas, theaters, and sports facilities, Jews were now forbidden from entering designated Aryan zones. Germany's existing anti-Semitic laws were expanded to ban Jews in professional life and to force Jews to publicly identify themselves with the Star of David on their clothing. Jews were now required to carry identification cards, and their passports were stamped with the letter "J." The Nazis also separated Jews from the non-Jewish German population by confining them to certain isolated neighborhoods. These neighborhoods, called ghettos, began to pop up all over Germany.

Some Jews began to realize that these measures were not designed to be temporary or a response to an emergency that would pass. The violence, hatred, and discrimination being directed against them were not going to stop. Some believed it would, in fact, only grow worse. Many German Jews fled to other countries, including Great Britain, France, and the United States. Immigration quotas based on these nations' own anti-Semitic sentiments limited the number of Jews who were able to escape Hitler's growing campaign to push Jews out of Germany.

When Hitler realized he could not rid Jews from Germany entirely through emigration, he began putting another plan in place. First, he created the ghettos, where Jews were forced to live and where their movement could be restricted. Soon, however, Hitler's methods of ridding Germany of its Jewish population would grow even more violent and depraved.

WAGING WORLD WAR II

As his army continued its segregation of and brutality against Jews, Hitler began to enforce a foreign policy aimed at incorporating into the Third Reich those ethnic Germans living outside the borders of Germany. The policy fueled Germany's goal of domination of western Europe and the acquisition of a vast new empire in eastern Europe to provide what Hitler called "living space," or Lebensraum. To accomplish these goals, Hitler realized he needed to go to war.

GERMANY INVADES POLAND, STARTS WORLD WAR II

In 1939, Hitler negotiated a pact with the Soviet Union, called the German-Soviet Pact (also referred to as the Ribbentrop-Molotov Pact) that had two significant parts. First, the pact ensured economic cooperation—Germany would exchange manufactured goods for Soviet raw materials. Second, both countries signed a ten-year nonaggression agreement in which each country promised not to attack the other.

After Hitler's invasion of Poland, the German Luftwaffe bombed the Polish capital of Warsaw. Hitler wanted to take control of Poland to further his mission of conquering all of Europe.

Knowing the Soviet Union would abide by this pact and not get involved, Germany attacked Poland on September 1, 1939. Hitler invaded Poland for two reasons. Parts of Poland had large German populations, and Hitler saw an opportunity to expand Germany's borders to encompass as many ethnic Germans as possible. This helped him realize his goal of Lebensraum—having a unified living space occupied only by Germans living on German soil. Hitler also had a military and economic reason for the invasion: he wanted to control a seaport in northern Poland, on the Danzig River, that served as an open corridor to transport goods and materials into and out of Germany.

Hitler's invasion hardly went unnoticed. Great Britain and France could no longer follow a policy of appeasement when it came to Hitler's continued aggression in Europe. Two days after the invasion, on September 3, Britain and France, which both had made promises of protection to Poland just five months earlier, declared war on Germany. World War II had begun.

Over the course of the next six years, a series of invasions and occupations took place all over Europe. Poland and eastern Europe were divided into Soviet and German spheres of interest. Germany invaded Norway and Denmark. The Soviet Union attacked Finland, while the Germans defeated France. The Soviet Union occupied and incorporated the Baltic states and seized several Romanian provinces. Germany began its assault on western Europe, attacking the Netherlands, Belgium, Luxembourg, and France. Japan entered the war by invading China. Italy invaded southern France and Greece.

THE UNITED STATES JOINS THE WAR

While World War II began in 1939, the United States did not join the war effort until after the Japanese—one of the Axis Powers that also included Germany and Italy—bombed an American naval fleet stationed in Pearl Harbor, Hawaii. On December 7, 1941, the Japanese staged a surprise air attack that began at 7:45 in the morning.

The Japanese attacked the U.S. Navy fleet in two stages. During the first stage, Japanese fighter planes bombed the

On December 7, 1941, the United States formally entered World War II when Japan bombed a U.S. military fleet stationed at Pearl Harbor, on the island of Oahu, Hawaii.

airfields, destroying aircraft and hampering initial efforts by the United States to respond to the attack. A second stage saw Japanese torpedo planes bombing U.S. battleships anchored along Ford Island. Several battleships were damaged, including the USS *Helena*, USS *Utah*, USS *Raleigh*, USS *California*, USS *Nevada*, USS *Oklahoma*, and USS *West Virginia*. The USS *Arizona* took a direct hit that caused an explosion, sinking the ship with more than 1,777 naval officers on board. Several U.S. aircraft carriers were out to sea and were able to respond to the attack, but not before the Pacific Fleet had been destroyed. The United States declared war on Japan on December 8, and on Germany and Italy three days later.

FRANKLIN D. ROOSEVELT'S "DAY OF INFAMY" SPEECH

"Yesterday, December 7th, 1941—a date which will live in infamy—the United States of America was suddenly and deliberately attacked by naval and air forces of the Empire of Japan. The United States was at peace with that nation, and, at the solicitation of Japan, was still in conversation with its government and its Emperor looking toward the maintenance of peace in the Pacific...

"The attack yesterday on the Hawaiian Islands has caused severe damage to American naval and military forces. I regret to tell you that very many American lives have been lost. In addition, American ships have been reported torpedoed on the high seas between San Francisco and Honolulu.

"Yesterday, the Japanese Government also launched an attack against Malaysia. Last night, Japanese forces attacked Hong Kong. Last night, Japanese forces attacked Guam. Last night, Japanese forces attacked the Philippine Islands. Last night, the Japanese attacked Wake Island. And this morning, the Japanese attacked Midway Island.

"Japan has therefore undertaken a surprise offensive extending throughout the Pacific area. The facts of yesterday and today speak for themselves. The people of the United States have already formed their opinions and well understand the implications to the very life and safety of our nation.

"As Commander-in-Chief of the Army and Navy, I have directed that all measures be taken for our defense, that always will our whole nation remember the character of the onslaught against us. No matter how long it may take us to overcome this premeditated invasion, the American people, in their righteous might, will win through to absolute victory. I believe that I interpret the will of the Congress and of the people when I assert that we will not only defend ourselves to the uttermost but will make it very certain that this form of treachery shall never again endanger us.

"Hostilities exist. There is no blinking at the fact that our people, our territory, and our interests are in grave danger. With confidence in our armed forces, with the unbounding determination of our people, we will gain the inevitable triumph. So help us God.

"I ask that the Congress declare that since the unprovoked and dastardly attack by Japan on Sunday, December 7th, 1941, a state of war has existed between the United States and the Japanese Empire."

– President Franklin D. Roosevelt, December 8, 1941 (Source: HistoryPlace.com)

ALLIED SOLDIERS ARRIVE

On June 6, 1944, as part of Operation Overlord, U.S., British, and Canadian troops landed on the beaches of Normandy, France. Under the command of U.S. general Dwight D. Eisenhower and British general Bernard Montgomery, an invasion force took on the Nazis. Supporting the Allied invasion were more than 155,000 American,

The Normandy Invasion, also called D-Day, marked the arrival of Allied soldiers to mainland Europe. U.S., British, and Canadian troops landed on the beaches of Normandy, France, on June 6, 1944, and steadily moved across Europe.

British, and Canadian troops; 50,000 vehicles; 7,000 naval ships; and 11,500 aircraft. Since the Normandy Invasion, June 6 has been known in World War II history as "D-Day" (in military jargon, D-Day is the day on which a combat attack or operation is to be initiated).

GERMANY SURRENDERS

As Allied troops moved across Europe in a series of invasions against the Nazis, they began to encounter concentration camps and tens of thousands of survivors. The Nazis, recognizing that they were being overpowered by Allied forces, began to evacuate these camps and force prisoners to march into the heart of Germany. These treks into the country were called death marches.

As Allied troops began to successfully fight their way through German-occupied Europe, the Nazis began to evacuate their concentration camps. Allied soldiers came across survivors and soon learned the horrors that occurred in the death camps.

Nazi soldiers did not want to abandon the prisoners for several reasons. The Nazis did not want survivors to tell their stories of what they had seen and experienced at the camps. In addition, the German army needed these prisoners for slave labor to continue producing weapons.

When Allied troops came upon death march prisoners, they found the survivors suffering from starvation and disease. Troops also discovered horrific and unspeakable conditions in the Nazi concentration camps. It was only after Allied troops started to liberate concentration camps that the full scope of the horrors perpetrated against Jews came to light, exposing the Nazis' actions to the world.

By the time World War II came to an end, more than fifty-five million lives—military and civilian—had been lost. Fought on six continents, World War II stands as the deadliest and most destructive war in history.

CHAPTER 3

THE HOLOCAUST: NAZI MASS MURDER

Throughout World War II, as the Nazis invaded neighboring countries and fought off the counterattacks of Allied forces, a controlled program of murder was taking place. Known as the Holocaust, this period of history was defined by an organized, government-sponsored initiative to persecute and murder between six and ten million Jews at the hands of the Nazi regime. The Nazis called their plan for the annihilation of Jews the "Final Solution."

Hitler played on the longstanding German-Christian fear and distrust of the Jewish religion. He pushed the idea that Jews, not Germans, were to blame for losing World War I and causing the subsequent economic collapse of the nation. Hitler and the Nazis believed that Germans were racially superior to all other ethnic groups, while Jews were both ethnically inferior and a threat to the German race's physical and moral purity. Jews, who were by far the most numerous victims of the Holocaust, were not alone in being targeted by the Nazis. Hitler also persecuted anyone whose politics, ideology, or behavior was perceived to be a threat to the Nazi regime or German purity. These included communists, socialists, Jehovah's Witnesses, homosexuals, and the disabled.

MURDER OF THE DISABLED

The Nazis' first systematic killing program targeted mentally and physically disabled people living in institutions within Germany and German-controlled territories. This Nazi initiative took place roughly two years before the beginning of the period of history known as the Holocaust.

The purpose of the Nazi "euthanasia" program was to eliminate those individuals whom the Nazis considered unworthy of life because they suffered from psychiatric,

Angela R.
2 Jahre

Annemarie D.
4 Jahre

Erika S.
3 Jahre

The Nazi euthanasia program targeted children, the disabled, and the mentally handicapped. Many of these victims' remains were used for medical research. The last two specimens were buried in the Central Cemetery in Vienna, Austria, in 2002. At a public service to honor the dead, young Austrians carried images of the many victims of the Nazis.

neurological, or physical disabilities. To the Nazis and Hitler, those suffering from mental or physical abnormalities were a financial burden to Germany. They also threatened Hitler's goal of establishing a pure race of Germans free of genetic mutations or supposed deficiencies.

Both children and adults were among those targeted. The Reich Ministry of the Interior began enforcing a decree that forced doctors, nurses, and midwives to report any newborn infant or child under the age of three who showed any signs of severe mental or physical disability. The children were classified according to the results of a questionnaire completed by medical staff. Children were not examined by doctors nor were their medical records reviewed.

Once a list of these children was created, health officials began encouraging the parents of these children to admit them to specially designated pediatric clinics located throughout Germany and Austria. These hospitals were not clinics that provided care for these children. Instead, they were killing wards where specially recruited medical staff murdered the children using lethal overdoses of medication or by starving them to death.

The program eventually expanded to include older children, adults, and the elderly suffering from mental or physical disabilities. By the time the program was shut down, more than one hundred thousand disabled children and adults had been murdered.

JEWISH GHETTOS

Jewish ghettos, or enclosed portions of German cities, were established to house Jews, who were forced to live under miserable conditions. The ghettos isolated Jews from the non-Jewish population and served as a place to hold and

A section of wall 8 feet (2.4 meters) high encircles a Jewish ghetto in Warsaw, Poland. Jews were forced to live in the ghettos, where health and sanitation were poor and disease spread quickly.

confine them while the Nazis decided how best to remove the Jewish population from Germany and German-occupied territory.

There were three types of ghettos: closed ghettos, open ghettos, and destruction ghettos. Most ghettos were closed ghettos, which were areas of a city that confined Jews with the use of walls and fences. Closed-off ghettos were extremely crowded, suffered from unsanitary conditions, and experienced chronic shortages of food and water. Many people starved.

Food and medical supplies were restricted in order to slowly kill off the Jewish residents. There also was inadequate heat provided during severe weather. Because so many people lived in unhealthy conditions, repeated outbreaks of disease caused many Jews to die.

Open ghettos had no walls or fences, but Jews living in these areas were restricted from coming and going freely. Destruction ghettos were sealed-off areas that existed for only a few weeks. Jews living in these ghettos were deported or killed quickly.

MOBILE KILLING SQUADS [*EINSATZGRUPPEN*]

When the Germans violated their nonaggression pact and invaded the Soviet Union in 1941, mobile killing units, called *einsatzgruppen*, followed the German army into the country. Their main goal was to kill Soviet Jews and any racial or political enemies, such as Roma (also known as gypsies) and officials of the Soviet state. Einsatzgruppen first targeted Jewish men, but later they also killed women and children. Jews were collected, often forcibly pulled out of their homes, and taken to execution sites where mass graves had been dug. Jews were shot and their bodies dumped into the graves.

Heinrich Himmler, a senior Nazi official and Reich leader of the Schutzstaffel, an elite, special police force that was responsible for guarding racial purity, began to notice the negative psychological effects that the mass killings were having on his guards. To alleviate the stress on his men, Himmler helped to create a mobile gas chamber that was housed in a cargo truck. The gas chamber was connected to the truck's exhaust pipes. The truck's exhaust, which was carbon monoxide, killed Jews forced into the truck. The guards no longer had to pull any triggers or directly witness any deaths.

CONCENTRATION CAMPS EXPAND

The first concentration camps were established in 1933, shortly after Hitler was appointed chancellor of Germany. As the Nazis began to conquer significant portions of Europe, more and more camps were needed to deal with prisoners of

U.S. officers inspect a gas chamber at a concentration camp. It is estimated that more than fifteen thousand concentration camps existed in Germany and Nazi-occupied countries.

war and those individuals and groups determined to be threats to the German nation. In addition to European Jews who lived in newly occupied countries, concentration camps also housed political prisoners, resistance groups, and other groups deemed racially inferior, such as the Roma (or gypsies).

Not only did the number of concentration camps grow, so, too, did their lethality and perversity. To more efficiently murder the growing number of concentration camp prisoners, the Nazis constructed gas chambers that could murder large groups of people at one time. Concentration camps were also used to conduct medical experiments on prisoners against their will. Some of these experiments included testing vaccines to fight against contagious diseases and determining how long a prisoner could survive in frozen water. The experiments were almost always fatal.

CONCENTRATION CAMPS

It is estimated that the Nazis had more than fifteen thousand concentration camps in Germany and countries occupied by German forces during World War II. Concentration camps served two key purposes. They were a source of forced labor for Nazi construction projects and for the production of weapons and other supplies for the German army. They were also used as brutally efficient death camps where millions of Jews and those perceived to be political or ideological threats to the Nazi philosophy were murdered. The list below is a sample of the more significant concentration camps established by the Nazis.

(continued on page 36)

(continued from page 35)

Camp	Location	Estimated Number of Murdered Jews
Auschwitz	Oswiecim, Poland	1,100,000
Belzec	Belzec, Poland	600,000
Bergen-Belsen	Hanover, Germany	35,000
Buchenwald	Buchenwald, Germany	No known estimate
Chelmno	Chelmno, Poland	320,000
Dachau	Dachau, Germany	32,000
Dora/Mittelbau	Sub-camp of Buchenwald, Germany	No known estimate
Drancy	Drancy, France	No known estimate
Flossenbürg	Flossenbürg, Germany	No known estimate
Gross-Rosen	Sub-camp of Sachsenhausen, Wroclaw, Poland	40,000
Janowska	L'viv, Ukraine	No known estimate
Kaiserwald/Riga	Meza-Park, Latvia	No known estimate
Koldichevo	Baranovichi, Belarus	22,000
Majdanek	Lublin, Poland	360,000
Mauthausen	Mauthausen, Austria	120,000
Natzweiler/Struthof	Natzweiler, France	12,000
Neuengamme	Sub-camp of Sachsenhausen, Hamburg, Germany	56,000
Plaszow	Krakow, Poland	8,000
Ravensbrück	Berlin, Germany	No known estimate
Sachsenhausen	Berlin, Germany	No known estimate
Sered	Sered, Slovakia	No known estimate
Sobibor	Sobibor, Poland	250,000
Stutthof	Danzig, Poland	65,000
Theresienstadt	Terezin, Czech Republic	33,000
Treblinka	Treblinka, Poland	No known estimate
Vaivara	Estonia	No known estimate
Westerbork	Westerbork, Netherlands	No known estimate

DEATH MARCHES AND CAMP LIBERATION

In 1944, the Soviet Union gained control of Belarus. Soviet forces took charge of the Lublin/Majdanek concentration camp, one of the Nazis' major camps. Upon learning of the takeover, Heinrich Himmler ordered that prisoners in all other concentration camps be evacuated and forced to walk into the middle of Germany, away from Allied forces that

These piles of discarded clothing belonged to prisoners held at the concentration camp at Dachau. Camp prisoners were forced to strip before they were killed.

were beginning to gain control over the borders of the country. Camp prisoners were forced to walk in harsh weather conditions while being savagely mistreated. Thousands of

A SURVIVOR'S STORY: BART STERN, LIBERATED FROM AUSCHWITZ

Bart Stern was a Hungarian Jew who had first been confined to a ghetto in his hometown, then deported to the Auschwitz extermination camp in Poland. In January 1945, as the Soviets advanced toward the camp near the end of the war, the Germans emptied most of Auschwitz and forced the prisoners into a death march. Stern hid and remained behind in the camp, along with a few inmates who were too ill to march. This is his survival and liberation story:

And it was by the greatest miracle that I survived… [W]hen they already left, the Germans, about an hour they, they left, there was no sign of Germans, I wanted to go back to the barracks, but the Poles, the, the Ukraines, who were not taken on the death march, they wouldn't let me in. So I was hiding out in the heap of dead bodies because in the last week when the crematoria didn't function at all, the bodies were just building up higher and higher. And I sneaked into, among those dead bodies because I was afraid they'd come back or something. So there I was at nighttime, in the daytime I was roaming around in the camp, and this is where I actually survived, January 27, I was one of the very first, Birkenau was one of the very first camps being liberated. This was my, my survival chance. (Source: United States Holocaust Memorial Museum)

camp prisoners died during the marches from exposure to the elements, starvation, or exhaustion. Many were shot to death if they collapsed or could no longer keep pace.

As U.S., British, and Soviet forces began to move across Europe, reclaiming lands that were occupied by Germany and the Nazis, soldiers began to come across thousands of prisoners who had survived the concentration camps and death marches. These survivors told the Allied troops that some prisoners were still being held in the camps. While the Nazis tried to destroy as much evidence of the horrific conditions at the camps as they could, Allied forces discovered proof of mass murder, such as gas chambers and warehouses filled with hundreds of thousands of personal items taken from camp prisoners. In some camps, Allied soldiers found piles of corpses that had not been buried.

NAZI OFFICIALS ARRESTED

As Allied forces seized control of Germany, Hitler, who did not want to be taken alive by Allied troops, killed himself in an underground bunker. Himmler, who was captured by Soviet troops, also committed suicide by ingesting a cyanide capsule he had hidden in his mouth before his capture. Even though the two top leaders of the Third Reich had avoided capture by taking their own lives, twenty-two other Nazi leaders and officials who had played key roles in orchestrating the Holocaust or in carrying out crimes against humanity were captured, arrested, and eventually stood trial.

AN INTERNATIONAL COURT CONVENES IN NUREMBERG

The Nazis surrendered to Allied forces in April 1945, ending Germany's involvement in World War II. In early August, Allied forces met in the German city of Potsdam and demanded the unconditional surrender of Japan, which ignored the request. In response, the United States dropped atomic bombs on the Japanese cities of Hiroshima and Nagasaki, effectively bringing the war to an official end.

In the weeks following the Nazi surrender, the question of how to deal with Nazi leaders arose. Twenty-two men, all of whom played major roles in orchestrating and carrying out the Holocaust, had been captured as a result of raids on concentration camps, Nazi headquarters, and other Nazi offices. They had each committed major war crimes and needed to be held accountable for their actions. While there was a significantly larger number of Nazi leaders and lower-level officials involved in the atrocities of the Holocaust, many fled Germany at the end of the war to avoid capture. This included hundreds of Nazis who came to the United States to live in hiding.

An Allied soldier stands guard over Albert Speer, Karl Doenitz, and Alfred Jodl, all Nazi leaders who were captured and later stood trial before the Nuremberg Tribunal.

THE WORLD SITS IN JUDGMENT

In October 1943, U.S. president Franklin D. Roosevelt, British prime minister Winston Churchill, and Soviet leader Joseph Stalin all signed the Moscow Declaration. It stated that those responsible for committing war crimes would be returned to their countries to be tried and judged according to that country's laws. It was decided that major war criminals, those who committed crimes that were so wide-spread, numerous, reprehensible, and atrocious, would be punished jointly by representatives of the Allied governments.

On August 8, 1945, the governments of the key Allied forces—the United States, the French Republic, the United Kingdom of Great Britain and Northern Ireland, and the Union of Soviet Socialist Republics—established the International Military Tribunal. The purpose of the tribunal was to try the perpetrators of the Holocaust in an open, international court of law and to hand down punishments for their crimes. The German city of Nuremberg was chosen as the site for the trials, which took place between 1945 and 1946. Judges were chosen from each of the major countries that formed the Allied forces.

Missing among the accused was Adolf Hitler and several of his closest aides, who had all committed suicide in the final days before Germany surrendered and the war itself came to an end. The tribunal's judges presided over the hearings of twenty-two major Nazi criminals:

- **Martin Bormann**, Hitler's assistant
- **Karl Doenitz**, German admiral who commanded the German navy
- **Hans Frank**, governor-general of Nazi-occupied Poland, called the "Jew butcher of Cracow"
- **Wilhelm Frick**, minister of the interior
- **Hans Fritzsche**, head of the Radio Division, one of twelve departments in the Propaganda Ministry
- **Walther Funk**, minister of economics
- **Hermann Goering**, Reichsmarschall and Luftwaffe (air force) chief; president of Reichstag; director of "Four Year Plan"

- **Rudolf Hess**, deputy to the Führer and Nazi Party leader
- **Alfred Jodl**, chief of operations for the German High Command
- **Ernst Kaltenbrunner**, chief of RSHA (an organization that included the offices of the Gestapo, the SD, and the Criminal Police) and chief of security police
- **Wilhelm Keitel**, chief of staff of the German High Command
- **Konstantin von Neurath**, minister of foreign affairs, then Reich protector for Bohemia and Moravia
- **Franz von Papen**, Reich chancellor prior to Hitler, vice chancellor under Hitler, and ambassador to Turkey
- **Erich Raeder**, commander-in-chief of the German navy
- **Joachim von Ribbentrop**, foreign minister
- **Alfred Rosenberg**, chief Nazi philosopher and Reichminister for the eastern occupied territories
- **Fritz Sauckel**, chief of slave labor recruitment
- **Hjalmar Schacht**, Reichsbank president and minister of economics
- **Baldur von Schirach**, Hitler Youth leader
- **Arthur Seyss-Inquart**, Austrian chancellor, then Reich commissioner for the Netherlands
- **Albert Speer**, Reichminister of armaments and munitions
- **Julius Streicher**, anti-Semitic editor of the Nazi newspaper *Der Stürmer*

EXCERPT OF OPENING STATEMENTS BY ROBERT H. JACKSON, CHIEF PROSECUTOR FOR THE UNITED STATES

"The privilege of opening the first trial in history for crimes against the peace of the world imposes a grave responsibility. The wrongs which we seek to condemn and punish have been so calculated, so malignant, and so devastating, that civilization cannot tolerate their being ignored, because it cannot survive their being repeated. That four great nations, flushed with victory and stung with injury stay the hand of vengeance and voluntarily submit their captive enemies to the judgment of the law is one of the most significant tributes that Power has ever paid to Reason…

"In the prisoners' dock sit twenty-odd broken men. Reproached by the humiliation of those they have led almost as bitterly as by the desolation of those they have attacked, their personal capacity for evil is forever past. It is hard now to perceive in these men as captives the power by which as Nazi leaders they once dominated much of the world and terrified most of it. Merely as individuals, their fate is of little consequence to the world.

"What makes this inquest significant is that these prisoners represent sinister influences that will lurk in the world long after their bodies have returned to dust. We will show them to be living symbols of racial hatreds, of terrorism and violence, and of the arrogance and cruelty of power. They are symbols of fierce nationalisms and of militarism, of intrigue and war-making which have embroiled Europe generation after generation, crushing its manhood, destroying its homes, and impoverishing its life. They have so identified themselves with the philosophies they conceived and with the forces they directed that any tenderness to them is a victory and an encouragement to all the evils which are attached to their names. Civilization can afford no compromise with the social forces which would gain renewed strength if we deal ambiguously or indecisively with the men in whom those forces now precariously survive…

"Civilization asks whether law is so laggard as to be utterly helpless to deal with crimes of this magnitude by criminals of this order of importance. It does not expect that you can make war impossible. It does expect that your juridical action will put the forces of international law, its precepts, its prohibitions, and, most of all, its sanctions, on the side of peace, so that men and women of good will, in all countries, may have 'leave to live by no man's leave, underneath the law.'" (Source: RobertHJackson.org)

THE PROSECUTION

Each of the four nations prosecuting Nazi war criminals at the Nuremberg Trials had their own judge, lead prosecutor and prosecutorial team of lawyers, researchers, and assistants. Each country was responsible for prosecuting one of four crimes.

The United States, led by chief prosecutor Robert H. Jackson, presented count one: conspiracy to wage aggressive war. This count addressed any crimes committed before World War II began or which indicated a defendant's plan to commit crimes during the war.

The British, represented by chief prosecutor Sir Hartley Shawcross, presented count two: crimes against peace. In essence, this count charged defendants with participating in planning and waging a war of aggression in violation of international treaties, arguments, and assurances. Shawcross served as Britain's attorney general.

Justice Robert H. Jackson, the lead prosecutor for the United States during the Nuremberg Trials, cross-examines a defendant.

Together, the French and Soviets presented counts three and four: war crimes and crimes against humanity. François de Menthon, the chief prosecutor representing France, was a former concentration camp inmate and a leader of the French Resistance. Roman A. Rudenko, the chief prosecutor representing the Union of Soviet Socialist Republics, was a Soviet lawyer who later became the U.S.S.R.'s prosecutor general. War crimes were defined as violations against the established rules for waging war. Crimes against humanity included inhumane acts committed against innocent people, civilians, or nonmilitary personnel, such as murder, extermination, enslavement, and deportation. These inhumane acts also included illegally seizing public or private property and the destruction of villages, cities, and towns that could not be justified by military necessity.

THE EVIDENCE AND VERDICTS

The four chief prosecutors of the Nuremberg Trials used the Nazis' own detailed records as the primary evidence

The Nazis looted hundreds of thousands of belongings from Jews, everything from jewelry (such as this box of wedding bands) to priceless pieces of art.

of the crimes committed. The prosecutors decided that the best, most compelling and convincing evidence of crimes committed by the defendants were their own words and actions.

Allied forces captured millions of documents during the last days of the war in 1945. Prosecutors submitted as evidence more than 3,000 tons of documents that outlined the crimes and atrocities committed by the defendants. This archive included:

- Documentation of Nazi-confiscated artwork, currency, and gold
- Documentation of Nazi policies, actions, and decisions
- Documentation regarding the progress of the mobile killing units
- Documentation regarding the cooperation of several German agencies in the Holocaust
- Documentation of orders to kill Jewish civilians during the Nazi invasion of the Soviet Republic
- Film and photographs of various Nazi activities, such as military invasions, mass murder, public humiliations of Jews, and activities that occurred at concentration camps

The documents, along with the film and photographs, provided powerful evidence of the crimes committed by the defendants.

Because the Nazis kept such precise records of their activities, most of the defendants had little choice but to admit their involvement in the crimes of which they were accused. As a matter of course, most of the accused claimed, as their defense, that they were only following the orders of a higher authority, meaning Hitler himself and other senior Nazi officials.

On October 1, 1946, the International Military Tribunal handed down its verdicts. Twelve of the defendants (Goering, Ribbentrop, Keitel, Kaltenbrunner, Rosenberg, Frank, Frick, Streicher, Sauckel, Jodl, Seyss-Inquart, and Bormann) were found guilty of being directly involved in killing innocent people. They received death sentences. Three (Hess, Funk, and Raeder) were sentenced to life in prison. Four (Doenitz, Schirach, Speer, and Neurath) received prison

Hermann Goering, Rudolf Hess, and Joachim von Ribbentrop listen to the verdict during their trial. Goering and Ribbentrop were found guilty on all four counts charged against them and sentenced to death. Hess was found guilty of two counts and sent to prison for life.

terms of up to twenty years. Three defendants (Schacht, Papen, and Fritzsche) were acquitted, or found innocent, of all charges.

For the defendants who received death sentences, the executions were carried out just fifteen days later. On October 16, 1946, they were hanged. The bodies of the executed men were brought to the concentration camp at Dachau where they were cremated in the same ovens that were used to burn victims of the Holocaust.

CHAPTER 5

A CLOSER LOOK AT THE DEFENDANTS

The defendants brought before the International Military Tribunal in Nuremberg all played significant roles in the Nazi Party, with many personally designing and perpetrating some of the most horrific of the atrocities committed against Jews and other Holocaust victims.

Martin Bormann served as the head of the party chancellery and as secretary to the Führer (Hitler). He was known to have a strong influence on Hitler. Bormann actively persecuted Jews and was linked to the orders that were given to enslave or kill people living in territories occupied by the Nazis. He was the only defendant tried in absentia, or while absent, from the Nuremberg Trials. He was missing until 1973, when West German authorities discovered and identified his remains.

Karl Doenitz was a German admiral who became commander-in-chief of the German navy. Personally chosen by Hitler as his successor, Doenitz negotiated the surrender of Nazi Germany to Allied forces after Hitler committed suicide. On the stand during the Nuremberg Trials, Doenitz said,

"Politicians brought the Nazis to power and started the war. They are the ones who brought about these disgusting crimes, and now we have to sit there in the dock with them and share the blame!" (as quoted by the University of Missouri-Kansas City School of Law).

Hans Frank was the governor-general of Nazi-occupied Poland and was referred to as the "Jew butcher of Cracow." He had a significant role in violently attacking Poland. He was also known to have overseen the first ghettos created to contain Jews.

Adolf Hitler stands with his private secretary Martin Bormann, who was known to have a strong influence on the Nazi leader. Bormann was the only defendant tried in absentia. In 1973, West German authorities discovered his remains.

Wilhelm Frick served as the minister of the interior and the Reichsprotektor of Bohemia and Moravia (the modern-day Czech Republic). As the minister of the interior, Frick had a role in planning the war. He also signed numerous orders for the killing of Jews and had direct knowledge of the torture committed against people living in mental institutions and hospitals.

Hans Fritzsche was a radio announcer who was later appointed as the head of the Wireless News Service for the Reich government. He was in charge of spreading pro-Nazi news and anti-Semitic messages against Jews. The

International Military Tribunal found he did not have any role in committing crimes against innocent people and as a result the Tribunal found him not guilty.

Walther Funk held the position of minister of economics, and in this role he was one of Hitler's most important economic advisers. As the minister of economics, Funk ordered Nazi soldiers to seize the personal possessions from Jews. When Funk was questioned on the stand, he admitted to his role in stealing Jewish possessions on behalf and in support of the Nazi Party, saying: "I signed the laws for the Aryanization of Jewish property. Whether that makes me legally guilty or not, is another matter. But it makes me morally guilty, there is no doubt about

Top Nazi Party members, including Adolf Hitler, Alfred Rosenberg (just behind Hitler to the left), and Hermann Goering (next to Hitler on the left), march during the fifteenth anniversary of the 1923 Beer Hall Putsch, an early, failed attempt by the Nazis to seize power.

that" (as quoted by the University of Missouri-Kansas City School of Law).

Hermann Goering was second in command to Hitler and held positions as Reichsmarschall and Luftwaffe chief, president of the Reichstag, and director of the Four Year Plan. He was sentenced to death, but on the day of his execution, Goering ingested a cyanide tablet and killed himself.

Rudolf Hess, deputy to the Führer and Nazi Party leader, was a personal aide to Hitler. He first met Hitler in 1924, when both men were serving prison sentences together. He supported Hitler until he escaped Germany for England at the end of the war. He was sentenced to life in prison and lived until the age of ninety-three. In May 1946, Hess wrote the following confession: "I declare herewith under oath that in the years 1941 to 1943, during my tenure in office as commandant of Auschwitz concentration camp, two million Jews were put to death by gassing and a half million by other means" (as quoted by the Holocaust Historiography Project).

Alfred Jodl was known as chief of operations and held a major role in the Nazis' invasions and occupations of Czechoslovakia, Norway, Greece, and Yugoslavia. He was sentenced to death for signing numerous documents that outlined plans to kill Jews and other Holocaust victims.

Ernst Kaltenbrunner was chief of the RSHA, an organization that included the offices of the Gestapo, the SD, and the Criminal Police. He also served as the chief of security police. He personally issued orders to kill Jews and was a key player in executing Hitler's Final Solution.

RESCUING EVIDENCE: THE ALFRED ROSENBERG DIARY

Alfred Rosenberg was an influential Nazi intellectual. When Hitler was imprisoned for his role in the Munich Beer Hall Putsch, Rosenberg took over as interim leader of the Nazi Party. Rosenberg authored a popular text called *The Myth of the Twentieth Century* (*Der Mythus des 20. Jahrhunderts*), which supported the Nazi idea of Aryan superiority and Jewish inferiority. The book pitted the "races" against one another.

After Hitler became chancellor of Germany, Rosenberg held numerous posts in the Nazi Party. Rosenberg was responsible for running the Nazis' art confiscation program, in which artwork, books, archival material, and other valuables were stolen from Jews and appropriated by the Nazi Party.

It was well known that Rosenberg kept a diary, which went missing after he was captured, tried during the Nuremberg Trials, and hanged for his role in the Holocaust. While the U.S. National Archives had obtained sections of the original diary and copies of other sections, it was not known what happened to the bulk of the diary after the war. Following clues regarding its location, the U.S. Holocaust Memorial Museum worked with the Federal Bureau of Investigation (FBI), the U.S. Department of Justice, and a private investigator to locate the diary.

In early 2013, the original diary was discovered by agents from the Homeland Security Investigations unit at a private company in upstate New York. The handwritten diary, with entries that date from 1936 to 1944, contains little-known facts about the Nazi Party, including the activities and interactions of the members of the top level of Nazi leadership. The diary will eventually be accessible to scholars and the public.

Wilhelm Keitel, who served as chief of staff of the Armed Forces High Command, was sentenced to death for his role in planning the war, issuing orders to kill communists, and guiding the invasion of the U.S.S.R.

Konstantin von Neurath served as minister of foreign affairs and Reich protector for Bohemia and Moravia. He was one of Hitler's primary military advisers.

Franz von Papen was at one time chancellor of Germany, prior to Hitler. When Hitler gained control of the country, Papen held several roles in the Third Reich, including ambassador to Turkey. Papen, however, did not play a role in planning the war, carrying out invasions, or participating in any efforts to kill Jews. The International Military Tribunal acquitted him. In explaining his conversations with Hitler, Papen said: "I think [Hitler] wanted the best for Germany at the beginning, but he became an unreasoning evil force with the flattery of his followers—Himmler, Goering, Ribbentrop, etc. ... I tried to persuade him he was wrong in his anti-Jewish policies many a time. He seemed to listen at first, but later on, I had no influence on him" (as quoted by the University of Missouri-Kansas City School of Law).

Erich Raeder, chief of naval command, admitted to violating the Versailles Treaty, a peace treaty instituted at the end of World War I. Raeder was charged with sinking a British passenger ship headed to America.

Joachim von Ribbentrop served as a foreign policy adviser to Hitler and ambassador to England. He was active in planning the Nazi attack of Poland and participating in Hitler's Final Solution. He was sentenced to death.

Alfred Rosenberg, a chief Nazi philosopher and Reichminister for the eastern occupied territories, was in charge of the Nazi Party while Hitler was in jail. He invaded more than seventy thousand Jewish homes in France, from which he confiscated art and other private property and personal possessions. He was also charged with participating in mass killings of Jewish people.

Fritz Sauckel was chief of slave labor recruitment and was responsible for creating slave labor, into which more than five million people had been forced.

Hjalmar Schacht was commissioner of currency, president of the Reichsbank, and minister of economics. While he was responsible for many economic decisions, Schacht did not play any direct role in crimes against humanity, plotting or carrying out the war, or participating in any form of killing.

Baldur von Schirach was Hitler's youth leader. He organized programs to recruit and train young men to become members of the Nazi Party and the German army. Schirach described his dedication and support of Hitler, saying: "I had no reason to be anti-Semitic...until someone made me read the American book, *The International Jew*, at the impressionable age of 17. You have no idea what a great influence this book had on the thinking of German youth. At the age of 18, I met Adolf Hitler. I must admit I was inspired by him...and became one of his staunchest supporters" (as quoted by the University of Missouri-Kansas City School of Law).

Arthur Seyss-Inquart was minister of security and the interior and served as the Austrian chancellor. He initiated a program to steal property from Jews and helped

Adolf Hitler discusses plans for a new provincial administration building with his chief architect, Albert Speer (in suit and tie).

establish economic discrimination policies against Jews living in the Netherlands.

Albert Speer, Reichminister of armaments and munitions, was known to be Hitler's chief architect and his personal friend. He was also very active in the slave labor program.

Julius Streicher was the editor of *Der Sturmer*, an anti-Semitic newspaper. He served as a spokesperson and

57

supporter of Hitler's plans for Jewish annihilation, and he played a significant role in spreading and encouraging anti-Semitic thoughts and behaviors. Streicher received a death sentence.

MORE BROUGHT TO JUSTICE

In the three years that followed the International Military Tribunal in Nuremberg, many more trials took place. Dozens of doctors, industrialists, members of the Nazi death squads, concentration camp guards, and others were tried for their roles in the Holocaust. In the years that followed, Nazi hunters searched for, identified, and discovered hundreds of Nazis who had fled Germany and were living in hiding. Some were even living out in the open. As these individuals were identified and their roles in the Holocaust were confirmed, they were brought to trial.

CHAPTER 6

SETTING AN INTERNATIONAL PRECEDENT

The Nuremberg Trials were groundbreaking for the precedents they set in international law. The trials helped to establish the notion that all of humanity could and would be safeguarded by laws that protected against not only the vicious attacks of individuals but also aggression and atrocities committed

Eleanor Roosevelt, widow of U.S. president Franklin D. Roosevelt, holds up a copy of the Universal Declaration of Human Rights, a document that emerged from the International Military Tribunal in Nuremberg. The Tribunal, for the first time, legally defined crimes against humanity.

59

by governments. This marked the first time in history that top officials from a nation were tried in an international court and held personally accountable for crimes committed in the name of their country or their government. It also established definitions for "war crimes" and "crimes against humanity" and marked the first time that these charges were levied against defendants and used in their prosecution.

ESTABLISHING INTERNATIONAL JUSTICE

The Nuremberg Trials established the first international criminal tribunal. They played a significant role in the drafting of human rights guarantees that would eventually become the Universal Declaration of Human Rights. The Nuremberg Tribunal also legally defined what constituted a crime against humanity. Numerous fundamental principles were also established, including:

- Individual responsibility for international crimes
- The right of the accused to have a fair trial
- The historic declaration that heads of state and high-level government officials were not guaranteed immunity from prosecution for crimes committed

The resulting changes to international law to include protection of human rights were profound, and the principles established by the Nuremberg Trials became universal. Indeed, the Nuremberg Trials became the basis for attempts to set up a permanent international court. As a result, the United Nations International Law Commission put forward the creation of a permanent court among its first proposals.

THE NUREMBERG PRINCIPLES

Created by the United Nations' International Law Commission in 1950, the Nuremberg Principles are a set of guidelines for international tribunals and courts to use when determining what constitutes a war crime. These principles are based upon the international legal principles established by the Nuremberg Trials. The complete text of the Nuremberg Principles follows (Source: International Committee of the Red Cross):

Principle I : Any person who commits an act which constitutes a crime under international law is responsible therefore and liable to punishment.

Principle II: The fact that internal law does not impose a penalty for an act which constitutes a crime under international law does not relieve the person who committed the act from responsibility under international law.

Principle III: The fact that a person who committed an act which constitutes a crime under international law acted as Head of State or responsible government official does not relieve him from responsibility under international law.

Principle IV: The fact that a person acted pursuant to order of his Government or of a superior does not relieve him from responsibility under international law, provided a moral choice was in fact possible to him.

Principle V: Any person charged with a crime under international law has the right to a fair trial on the facts and law.

Principle VI: The crimes hereinafter set out are punishable as crimes under international law:

(a) Crimes against peace:

(i) Planning, preparation, initiation, or waging of a war of aggression or a war in violation of international treaties, agreements, or assurances;

(continued on page 62)

(continued from page 61)

(ii) Participation in a common plan or conspiracy for the accomplishment of any of the acts mentioned under (i).

(b) War crimes:

Violations of the laws or customs of war which include, but are not limited to, murder, ill-treatment, or deportation to slave labor or for any other purpose of civilian population of or in occupied territory; murder or ill-treatment of prisoners of war or persons on the Seas, killing of hostages, plunder of public or private property, wanton destruction of cities, towns, or villages, or devastation not justified by military necessity.

(c) Crimes against humanity:

Murder, extermination, enslavement, deportation, and other inhumane acts done against any civilian population, or persecutions on political, racial, or religious grounds, when such acts are done or such persecutions are carried on in execution of or in connection with any crime against peace or any war crime.

Principle VII: Complicity in the commission of a crime against peace, a war crime, or a crime against humanity, as set forth in Principle VI, is a crime under international law.

SHE IS...

KIDNAPPED.
PROCURED ILLEGALLY

A young woman protests human trafficking in Bangalore, India.

Many of the countries that were occupied by Germany during World War II, including Poland, the former Czechoslovakia, the Soviet Union, Hungary, Romania, and

France, all held their own war crimes trials, as did the United States and Britain. These included the Auschwitz, Dachau, and Belsen trials, among others. In these national courts, the Nazis who persecuted civilian populations, along with those local officials and citizens who collaborated with the Germans, were brought to trial. Hundreds of thousands of defendants have been tried since the end of World War II.

THE UNIVERSAL DECLARATION OF HUMAN RIGHTS

Adopted by the United Nations General Assembly on December 10, 1948, the Universal Declaration of Human Rights outlines the rights to which all human beings are entitled. The Nuremberg Trials set an early precedent for this kind of declaration that enshrines the most basic freedoms and protections due to every single individual, no matter where he or she lives, and in no matter what circumstances or conditions. The document contains thirty articles that set forth these universal human rights. A sample of these rights include the following:

- Everyone is entitled to rights and freedoms without regard for race, color, sex, language, religious affiliation, political association, or national or social origin.
- No individual will be held as a slave of any kind, to anyone.
- No person will be tortured or will endure any form of degrading treatment or punishment.
- All people are equal under the law, and all are entitled to equal protection under these laws.

Ramiza Gurdic, a Bosnian Muslim woman, is a survivor of the 1995 Srebrenica massacre. She watches on television as the former Bosnian Serb army commander, Ratko Mladic, is tried before an international court for crimes against humanity and various other war crimes.

- Everyone is entitled to a fair and public trial to determine guilt for charges raised against them.

Observance of and respect for the Universal Declaration of Human Rights has varied. Atrocities continue to be committed around the world, including genocide and mass murder in countries like Rwanda, the Congo, Bangladesh, Uganda, Iraq, Indonesia, East Timor, El Salvador, Burundi, Argentina, Somalia, Chad, and the former Yugoslavia, among others. Prosecution of war crimes following these atrocities has often been a long, arduous, frustrating, and incomplete process. The quest to protect and guarantee justice for all the world's peoples continues.

Timeline

1914–1918 World War I devastates Europe.

January 30, 1933 Adolf Hitler appointed chancellor of Nazi Germany; citizens stripped of basic rights and many freedoms; anti-Semitic discrimination and persecution begins.

August 23, 1939 Nazi Germany and the Soviet Union sign a nonaggression pact and secretly agree to divide eastern Europe.

September 1, 1939 Germany invades Poland.

September 3, 1939 Great Britain and France declare war on Germany.

July 10, 1940–October 31, 1940 The Battle of Britain ends in defeat for Nazi Germany.

September 27, 1940 Germany, Italy, and Japan sign the Tripartite Pact.

June 22, 1941–November 1941 Nazi Germany and its Axis partners invade the Soviet Union.

December 7, 1941 Japan bombs Pearl Harbor, Hawaii.

December 8, 1941 The United States declares war on Japan, entering World War II.

December 11–13, 1941 Nazi Germany and its Axis partners declare war on the United States.

June 4, 1944 Allied troops liberate Rome; within two months, American and British bombers are able to hit targets in eastern Germany for the first time.

June 6, 1944 D-Day: British and U.S. troops land on the beaches of Normandy, France.

December 16, 1944 The Battle of the Bulge is Germany's final attempt to re-conquer Belgium and weaken Allied forces.

January 1, 1945 The Germans retreat following defeat in the Battle of the Bulge.

April 30, 1945 Hitler commits suicide.

May 7, 1945 Germany surrenders to the western Allies.

August 6, 1945 The United States drops an atomic bomb on Hiroshima, Japan.

August 8, 1945 The International Military Tribunal is established.

August 9, 1945 The United States drops an atomic bomb on Nagasaki, Japan.

September 2, 1945 Japan surrenders; World War II ends.

October 6, 1945 Leading Nazi officials indicted for war crimes.

October 1, 1946 The International Military Tribunal announces its verdicts.

October 6, 1946 Defendants sentenced to death are hanged.

Glossary

ACQUIT To decide that someone is not guilty of a crime.

ALLIED POWERS The countries (United States, Great Britain, France, U.S.S.R.) that opposed the Axis powers during World War II.

ANTI-SEMITISM Prejudice, hatred of, or discrimination against Jews.

ARYANIZATION The forced transfer of Jewish-owned businesses to non-Jewish people in Nazi Germany and Nazi-occupied territories.

AXIS POWERS The countries (Germany, Japan, Italy) that opposed the Allied powers during World War II.

CHANCELLOR Head of a government.

DECREE An official order given by a person with power and authority or by a government.

EUTHANASIA The act or practice of killing or permitting the death of hopelessly sick or injured individuals.

FOREIGN POLICY Self-interest strategies chosen by a nation to safeguard its national interests and to achieve its goals within international relations.

FÜHRER A German word meaning "leader."

GHETTO A neighborhood that contained and limited the movement of Jews in Nazi Germany and Nazi-occupied territories.

HOLOCAUST A word of Greek origin meaning "sacrifice by fire." The period of history where millions of Jews were murdered by the Nazis.

INDICTMENT An official written statement charging a person with a crime.

LEBENSRAUM Hitler's policy of creating a living space in Germany occupied only by ethnic Germans.

MEIN KAMPF An autobiographical book written by Hitler that outlines his theories and plans for a unified Germany.

POGROM A violent massacre or persecution of an ethnic or religious group; historically, Jewish communities have been victims of pogroms.

PROPAGANDA Ideas or statements that are often false or exaggerated and that are spread in order to support and sustain a cause, a political leader, or a government.

PROSECUTOR A lawyer who represents the side in a court case that accuses a person, group of people, company, organization, or government of a crime and who tries to prove that person's or group's guilt.

RACISM Actions, practices, or beliefs that consider the human species to be divided into races with shared traits, abilities, or qualities, and especially the belief that races can be ranked as inherently superior or inferior to others, or that members of different races should be treated differently.

TRIBUNAL Any person or institution with the authority to judge, adjudicate on, or determine claims or disputes.

VERDICT The finding, decision, judgment, or verdict of a jury on the matter submitted to it in a trial.

For More Information

Anne Frank Center USA
44 Park Place
New York, NY 10007
(212) 431-7993
Web site: http://www.annefrank.com
The Anne Frank Center USA educates young people
   about the dangers of intolerance, anti-Semitism,
   racism, and discrimination.

Los Angeles Museum of the Holocaust
100 South The Grove Drive
Los Angeles, CA 90036
(323) 651-3704
Web site: http://www.lamoth.org
The Los Angeles Museum of the Holocaust commemo-
   rates those who perished and those who survived by
   housing the precious artifacts that miraculously
   weathered the Holocaust era.

Project Witness
207 Foster Avenue
Brooklyn, NY 11230
718-WITNESS (948-6377)
Web site: http://www.projectwitness.org
Project Witness provides groundbreaking resources for
   Holocaust education while remaining deeply commit-
   ted to a unique mission: exploring the spiritual,

ethical, and intellectual responses of Holocaust survivors and victims.

U.S. Holocaust Memorial Museum
100 Raoul Wallenberg Place SW
Washington, DC 20024-2126
(202) 488-0400
Web site: http://www.ushmm.org
The U.S. Holocaust Memorial Museum inspires citizens
    and leaders worldwide to confront hatred, prevent
    genocide, and promote human dignity.

Vancouver Holocaust Education Centre
#50-950 West 41st Avenue
Vancouver, BC V5Z 2N7
Canada
(604) 264-0499
Web site: http://www.vhec.org
The Vancouver Holocaust Education Centre's goal is to
    leave a permanent legacy devoted to Holocaust-based
    anti-racism education.

Wiener Library for the Study of the Holocaust and Genocide
29 Russell Square
London WC1B 5DP
England
Tel.: +44 (0) 20 7636 7247
Web site: http://www.wienerlibrary.co.uk

The Wiener Library is one of the world's leading and most extensive archives on the Holocaust and Nazi era. Formed in 1933, the library's unique collection of over one million items includes published and unpublished works, press cuttings, photographs, and eyewitness testimony.

Yad Vashem
Har Hazikaron
P.O. Box 3477
Jerusalem, Israel 910340
Web site: http://www.yadvashem.org
Yad Vashem was established in 1953 as the world center for documentation, research, education, and commemoration of the Holocaust.

WEB SITES

Due to the changing nature of Internet links, Rosen Publishing has developed an online list of Web sites related to the subject of this book. This site is updated regularly. Please use this link to access the list:

http://www.rosenlinks.com/DHH/Nurem

For Further Reading

Altman, Linda Jacobs. *Shattered Youth in Nazi Germany.* Berkeley Heights, NJ: Enslow Publishers, 2010.

Bascomb, Neal. *The Nazi Hunters: How a Team of Spies and Survivors Captured the World's Most Notorious Nazi.* New York, NY: Arthur A. Levine Books, 2013.

Byers, Ann. *Rescuing the Danish Jews: A Heroic Story from the Holocaust.* Berkeley Heights, NJ: Enslow Publishers, 2011.

Byers, Ann. *Youth Destroyed: The Nazi Camps.* Berkeley Heights, NJ: Enslow Publishers, 2010.

Darmen, Peter. *The Holocaust and Life Under Nazi Occupation.* New York, NY: Rosen Publishing, 2012.

Deem, James M. *Kristallnacht: The Nazi Terror That Began the Holocaust.* Berkeley Heights, NJ: Enslow Publishers, 2011.

Doswell, Paul. *Story of the Second World War.* London, England: Usborne Books, 2010.

Fishkin, Rebecca Love. *Heroes of the Holocaust.* North Mankato, MN: Compass Point Books, 2011.

Fitzgerald, Stephanie. *Children of the Holocaust.* North Mankato, MN: CompassPoint Books, 2011.

Haugen, David, and Susan Musser. *The Holocaust.* Farmington Hills, MI: Greenhaven Press, 2011.

Janeczko, Paul B. *Requiem: Poems of the Terezin Ghetto.* Somerville, MA: Candlewick Press, 2013.

Kaufman, Lola Rein, and Lois Metzger. *The Hidden Girl: A True Story of the Holocaust.* New York, NY: Scholastic Paperbacks, 2010.

Kor, Eva Mozes, and Lisa Rojany Buccieri. *Surviving the Angel of Death: The True Story of a Mengele Twin in Auschwitz.* Terre Haute, IN: Tanglewood Press, 2012.

Laskier, Rutka, Daniella Zaidman-Mauer, and Kelly
    Knauer. *Rutka's Notebook: A Voice from the Holocaust*. New
    York, NY: Time Inc. & Yad Vashem, 2008.
Price, Sean Stewart. *A Wicked History: Adolf Hitler*. London,
    England: Franklin Watts, 2010.
Rappaport, Doreen, Emily Beresford, and Jeff Crawford.
    *Beyond Courage: The Untold Story of Jewish Resistance During
    the Holocaust*. Grand Haven, MI: Candlewick on
    Brilliance Audio, 2012.
Sheehan, Sean. *Why Did the Holocaust Happen?* New York,
    NY: Gareth Stevens Publishing, 2010.
Stille, Darlene. *Architects of the Holocaust*. North Mankato,
    MN: CompassPoint Books, 2011.
Wagner, Melissa. *The Big Book of World War II*. New York,
    NY: Perseus Books Group, 2009.
Witterick, J. L. *My Mother's Secret: Based on a True Holocaust
    Story*. Bloomington, IN: iUniverse, 2013.

Bibliography

Beck, Roger B., et al. *World History: Patterns of Interaction*. Boston, MA: McDougal Littell, 2008.

Cohen, Patricia. "Diary of a Hitler Aide Resurfaces After a Hunt That Lasted Years." *New York Times*, June 13, 2013. Retrieved October 2013 (http://www.nytimes.com /2013/06/14/world/europe/diary-of-a-hitler-aide-resurfaces-after-a-hunt-that-lasted-years.html?_r=0).

Conot, Robert E. *Justice at Nuremberg*. New York, NY: Basic Books, 1993.

Ehrenfreund, Norbert. *The Nuremberg Legacy: How the Nazi War Crimes Trials Changed the Course of History*. New York, NY: Palgrave Macmillan, 2007.

HistoryPlace.com. "Day of Infamy Speech." Retrieved October 2013 (http://www.historyplace.com/speeches /fdr-infamy.htm).

HistoryPlace.com. "Nazi Euthanasia." Retrieved October 2013 (http://www.historyplace.com/worldwar2 /holocaust/h-euthanasia.htm).

HistoryPlace.org. "Triumph of Hitler: The Nuremberg Laws." Retrieved December 2013 (http://www.historyplace.com/ worldwar2/triumph/tr-nurem-laws.htm).

Holocaust Historiography Project. "Rudolf Hess: Pillar of the Holocaust Extermination Thesis." Retrieved December 2013 (http://www.historiography-project.com/misc/ hoess.html).

International Committee of the Red Cross. "Principles of International Law Recognized in the Charter of the Nuremberg Tribunal and in the Judgment of the

Tribunal, 1950." Retrieved December 2013 (http://www.icrc.org/ihl/INTRO/390).

JewishVirtualLibrary.org. "Excepts from *Mein Kampf.*" Retrieved October 2013 (http://www.jewishvirtual library.org/jsource/Holocaust/kampf.html).

Persico, Joseph E. *Nuremberg: Infamy on Trial.* New York, NY: Penguin Books, 1995.

RobertHJackson.org. "Opening Statements Before the International Military Tribunal." Retrieved November 2013 (http://www.roberthjackson.org/the-man/speeches-articles/speeches/speeches-by-robert-h-jackson/opening-statement-before-the-international-military-tribunal).

Roland, Paul. *The Nuremberg Trials: The Nazis and Their Crimes Against Humanity.* London, England: Arcturus Publishing Ltd., 2012.

Tusa, Ann, and John Tusa. *The Nuremberg Trial.* New York, NY: Skyhorse Publishing, 2010.

United Nations. "The Universal Declaration of Human Rights." Retrieved October 2013 (http://www.un.org/en/documents/udhr).

U.S. Holocaust Memorial Museum. "The Alfred Rosenberg Diary." Retrieved October 2013 (http://www.ushmm.org/information/exhibitions/online-features/special-focus/the-alfred-rosenberg-diary).

U.S. Holocaust Memorial Museum. "Death Marches." Retrieved October 2013 (http://www.ushmm.org/wlc/en/article.php?ModuleId=10005162).

U.S. Holocaust Memorial Museum. "German Foreign Policy, 1933-1945." Retrieved October 2013 (http://www.ushmm.org/wlc/en/article.php?ModuleId=10005203).

U.S. Holocaust Memorial Museum. "Liberation of Nazi Camps." Retrieved October 2013 (http://www.ushmm.org/wlc/en/article.php?ModuleId=10005131).

U.S. Holocaust Memorial Museum. "Liberation of Nazi Camps—Oral History: Bart Stern." 1992. Retrieved November 2013 (http://www.ushmm.org/wlc/en/media_oi.php?ModuleId=10005131&MediaId=1100).

U.S. Holocaust Memorial Museum. "Nuremberg Defendants." Retrieved October 2013 (http://www.ushmm.org/wlc/en/article.php?ModuleId=10007654).

University of Missouri-Kansas City School of Law. "Charter of the International Military Tribunal." Retrieved October 2013 (http://law2.umkc.edu/faculty/projects/ftrials/nuremberg/NurembergIndictments.html).

University of Missouri-Kansas City School of Law. "Defendants in the Major War Figures Trial." Retrieved October 2013 (http://law2.umkc.edu/faculty/projects/ftrials/nuremberg/meetthedefendants.html).

Index

ABOUT THE AUTHOR

Laura La Bella is the author of more than twenty-five nonfiction children's books. She has written numerous books that examine humanitarian efforts, international affairs, and global concerns, including a profile of actress and activist Angelina Jolie in *Angelina Jolie: Goodwill Ambassador to the UN*; a report on the declining availability of the world's fresh water supply in *Not Enough to Drink: Pollution, Drought, and Tainted Water Supplies*; and a survey of the food industry in *Safety and the Food Supply*. La Bella lives in Rochester, New York, with her husband and son.

PHOTO CREDITS

Cover (clockwise from top left) Popperfoto/Getty Images, David E. Scherman/Time Life Pictures/Getty Images, © iStockphoto.com/Steve Christensen, Popperfoto/Getty Images, Keystone/Archive Photos/Getty Images; pp. 4–5 Galerie Bilderwelt/Hulton Archive/Getty Images; pp. 8–9 FPG/Archive Photos/Getty Images; p. 10 Roger Viollet/Getty Images; pp. 14, 23 Keystone/Hulton Archive/Getty Images; p. 18 Popperfoto/Getty Images; p. 21 Underwood Photo Archives/SuperStock; pp. 26, 30, 49, 62 © AP Images; pp. 27, 34 Keystone-France/Gamma-Keystone/Getty Images; p. 32 Library of Congress Prints and Photographs Division; pp. 37, 47 National Archives/Hulton Archive/Getty Images; pp. 41, 51 Mondadori/Getty Images; p. 46 Ralph Morse/Time & Life Pictures/Getty Images; p. 52 Hugo Jaeger/Time & Life Pictures/Getty Images; p. 57 Hulton Archive/Getty Images; p. 59 Fotosearch/Archive Photos/Getty Images; p. 64 Elvis Barukcic/AFP/Getty Images; cover and interior page background elements optimarc/Shutterstock.com (gray textures), Gallup Pix/Photodisc/Thinkstock (pillars), Gubin Yury/Shutterstock.com (barbed wire).

Designer: Nicole Russo; Photo Researcher: Cindy Reiman